Fortune Cookies

Volume 6

Dr. Kareem Pottinger

YSD Publishing House

Library of Congress Catalog in Publication Data

YSD PUBLISHING HOUSE
14490 Coastal Bay Circle 13204
Naples, FL. 34119

Library of Congress Catalog Card Number:
2013934185
International Standard Book Number 978-1-937171-05-6

Dedicated to my firstborn

YOUNGSABATH POTTINGER

If I ever leave this planet, I have
always kept you in mind.

Not leavening my wisdom far behind

Grow Good

INTRODUCTION

The true intent of this book
was to write a set of guidelines
that could be
immediately implemented in
the progress and advancement
of my sons elite
life.
This vast deep knowledge was
to be used as a
tool
to keep him far beyond just,
"ahead of the learning curb" for
lack of better expression.
These
rules are the widely accepted
and used unspoken
secrets amongst the elite in
which we use to rear our

young.
Although these are our secrets
and most of us will and should be extremely displeased for having them on display for the "normal's" of the world to receive, I decided to release them nevertheless.
For,
upon reading the finished piece I realized that these elite secrets
could not only serve to benefit my son and family to come well, but that the entire world
could serve to benefit from these lists of guidelines.
The way that this book is intended to be received is to

ponder upon each page for a complete 24 hours.

Each page is to be pondered upon for the whole day; it is to be used as topic of discussion for that day amongst peers, friends, and family members' etcetera.

It is especially designed to be pondered upon mostly by you. For a complete 24 hours deep thought on each subject should be pondered upon. The reason being is to see how these guidelines could be implemented into your current life, how should they have been implemented in your past life, and how can they benefit your future.

It
is only through the true
belief
and usage of these
guidelines
that your life's
works will be greatly
affected
in its progress.

*In life you
have
to
feed and water
the
sprouts
that you
would
like
to
see
grow*

*Depending
upon how
important you
are to any
particular
project
will always be
the decision
maker whether
you are to be
sacrificed
or not*

*Your initial
direct-action
will
always
be
faster
than a
response
which
is
a
reaction*

*It will always
be up to you
to
decide
who
you
are
and
will
become
in
this life*

The accomplishment of a goal which you set out to do, the success in that accomplishment can give you a confidence that you never knew you could posses

*Understand
that whoever
is sitting in the
driver-seat
of any
particular aim,
goal, or, project
can choose
to be very
selective; it is
their right
to do so*

When it is a
tough-road
ahead;
you really
need to believe
in your idea
and
stick with it
in order
to get through
the
journey

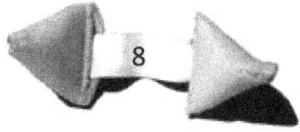

Most of the people in this world will need the feeling of a routine, they will need to be stuck in a certain type of rut which naturally works for them; which is why they are timid of anyone that runs independently free from these ruts or routines

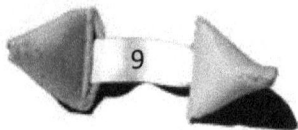

*The irony
of the
easy-way
is that
it
usually
takes
a lot
longer
to
accomplish
things*

*Other
peoples
definition
of you
when giving
a
description
are more
about
making
themselves
feel better*

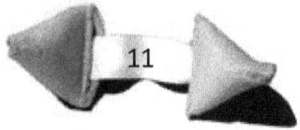

Always be
worthy
of
respect
and
you
will never
have anything
to
hold your
head-down
about

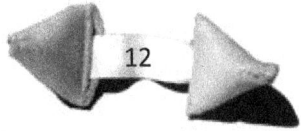

*It will always
be
best for you
to
stick-with
the
person or
persons
that
understands
you
the most*

*Leaving
things
up
to
fate
will
always
be
for
the
lazy*

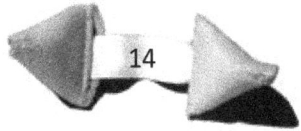

*You can
try to
throw
your
reputation
away
but it
will
always
come back
to
you*

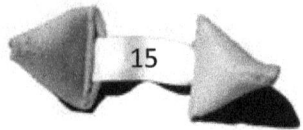

*With
enough
tenacity
you
can
make
almost
any
wrong
a
right*

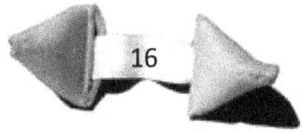

You
should
not
keep
things
around
unless
you
plan
to
use
them

*You shouldn't
ever depend on
others
to
make your
dreams
come
true when you
really would
like for those
dreams to come
true*

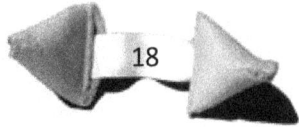

*It is very
important for
you to
understand
that as a
collective-whole
everyone
cannot all be
wrong
at
the
same-time*

*Always try
to
accentuate
your
positive
and this will
always give
you the
ability to put
your
best-foot
forward*

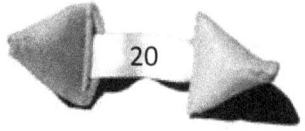

*People
will
only
see
what
you
allow
them
to
see*

*Understand
that you make
your own
luck
in this
world
and that's
going to be
either
good-luck
or
tough-luck*

*A
good-map
will
always
get
you
where
you
need
to
go*

*Each and every
person
that you are
making an
assessment
about
should
be
judged
on
their
own-merits*

*The
clarity
that
you
possess
in your
mind
can never
be
a
bad
thing*

*Do things
right
the
first-time
and
you will
never
have to
do
them
over
again*

It is extremely
important
for
you
to
leave
the
peasant
things
to
the
peasants

When you are trying to amass any type of wealth; you have to make money work for you, you are never going to make any substantial amount of money working for money

*Life
is
too
short
to
just
give-up
on
yourself*

*In order
to create
wealth
you
have
to
do
more
of
the
right
thing*

Sometimes
a
situation
is
not
great
but
it
is
not
bad
either

The type of freedom that you will receive from financial independence will help you to realize your full-potential which is why it is so important for you to arrive at the level of financial independence

Most times
when you are
reaching for
that
next-level
you will
have to take a
few chances;
everything in
this life is not
always written
in stone

*It is important
for you
to
understand
that
in order
for you to
win,
trade-offs
will
always have to
be made*

When

you

don't

know

the

truth

you

cannot

protect

yourself

from

error

*When
dealing
with
people
it is
important to
remember
that
not
everyone
has
vision*

Confidence
will
always
be
the
name
of
a
winners
game

*Eat
first,
sing
later*

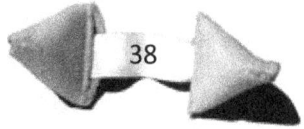

*There are
many
situations in life
that
are a lot
easier for you
to get
into
than
it will be for
you to get out
of*

*The only way
for you to
get
something
that you want
will be
for you
to go out
into
the world
and
get-it*

*When you
do not leave
room
for
mistakes
you can not
do anything
about it
when
you
run
into them*

*In order
to streamline
the
achievement in
the task that
you have to
accomplish, you
will have to
focus in on
exactly what is
important in
that task*

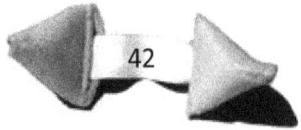

*Have the
wisdom
to
recognize
useful
discoveries
that can be
used to your
advantage
and
you will always
prosper*

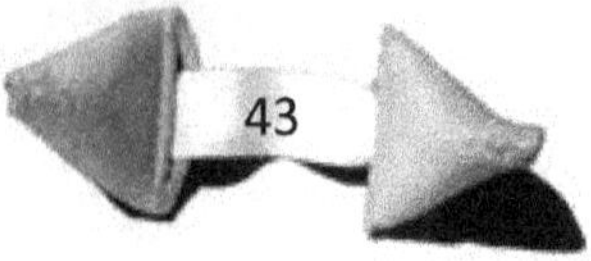

*Be
careful
of
hitting
a
home-run
and
not
even
knowing
it*

You should never leave your things in the hands of a person who does not understand the value of the personal effort it took to achieve those things

*High
levels
have
thoughts
which
live
in
high
places*

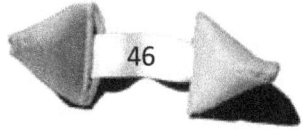

*The
indicator
for you to take
the
risk or not
should
always
be whether the
reward
is
well worth
the risk*

*Once
you finally
decide to
take action and
you do so, you
will see that
everything
that you do
towards that
goal will fall
into its
place*

48

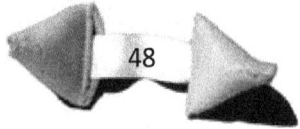

*If you
wont
take
your
life
serious
who
will
take it
serious
for
you*

Whoever you think that you are and are aiming to become; is what direction your life will be pointed into in order for you to become that person, so be very sure that it is the lifestyle that you really want

*Always
remember
that
it
only
takes
one
person
to
end
a
good-thing*

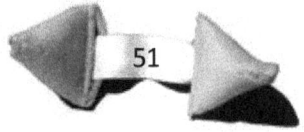

*As long as you
are making
progress
in your
task
when there is
a long way to
go,
that is what
really counts
and is truly
important*

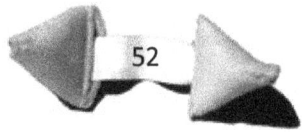

Your performance will always be a reflection of how you take care of yourself

53

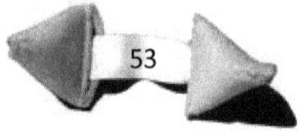

*Sweat
and
hustle
are
what
dreams
are
made
out
of*

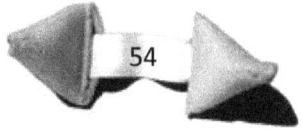

*Be
prepared
for
what
you
wish
for
because
you
just
might
get it*

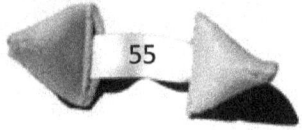

*Anyone
in
your
life
that you
have
deemed
unnecessary
needs
to be
banished
immediately*

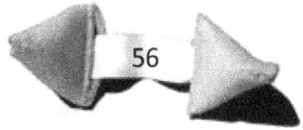

*It takes
a
tremendous
amount
of
will and
inner-resource
to keep on
going
when things
get
truly-tough*

Always do the best with what you have and you will never be disappointed by your performance

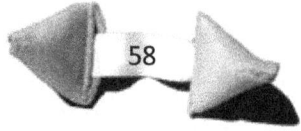

You could have
all the
talent
in the
world
and it will not
mean
anything if you
are
playing
the
wrong-game

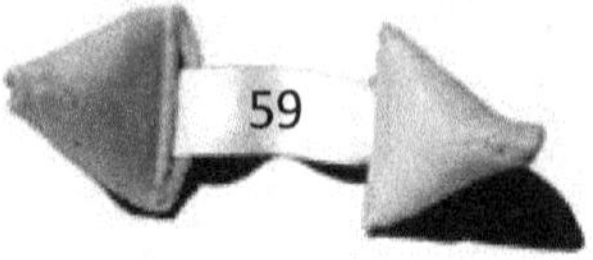

*Never
forget
that
some
people
who
you
will
encounter
are
just
simpletons*

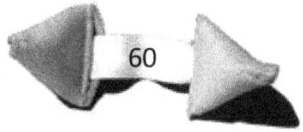

*The exposure
to the
worlds'
best
of the
best
is what
you
should desire
and always
be
seeking*

*When trying
to
attain
large
success
it is
really
important
to
keep-up
your
public-image*

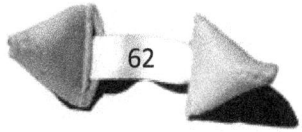

Use

your

head

for

something

other

than

just

growing

hair

The
only
cure
for
losing
everything
is
to
acquire
new
things

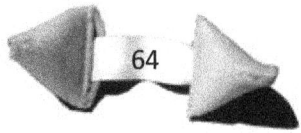

*Love
shines
brightest
when
it
is
in
the
dark*

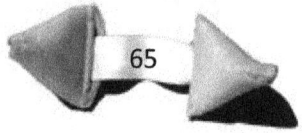

*Don't ever stop
your pursuit
to
obtain
more in life,
there will
always be
something
more for
you to see
and
to do*

*The most
challenging
goals
will always
be the most
difficult
to
secure
but also the
most uplifting
when
accomplished*

The information
that you
posses
which another
does not
is so
powerful
that it
will
always
up
your-ante

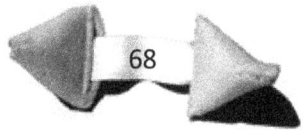

You will
always
be
weak
until
you
learn
how
to
take
control

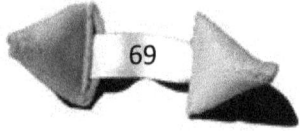

*You
must
stretch
the
limits
when
you
want
to
be
profitable*

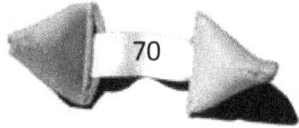

Personal travel
teaches you
more about
a
subject
than
any
book,
conversation,
or
school
ever can

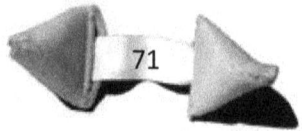

When you
start
paying
attention to
fear,
that
is
when
you start
heading-down
the
wrong-road

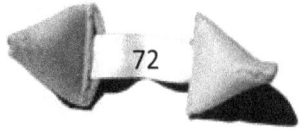

*If you
don't follow
through
on
your
dreams;
then why
are you
here on
earth, this
should be your
next question*

*The
real
crime
happens
when
you
do
not
finish
what
you
can*

To succeed
and
not obtain the
feeling of
fulfillment
is
because
you did not
align your goals
with
what you
truly-value

What is your
strategy
of getting to
the
point
in your
life
where you
feel
you have
made
it

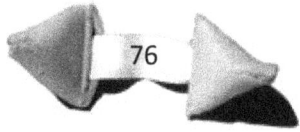

*It is
unfortunate
but some
people will
only see
and hear
the bad
things when it
comes time to
taking a chance
for greater
opportunities*

To fallback will always be easier than stepping-up to conquer a challenge which is why most people in their life will never complete anything of substantial value

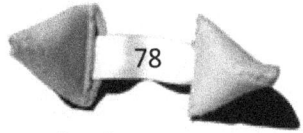

*Opportunities
are seldom
perfect
and when
you are
not ready
for them
they
may
never
come
back-around*

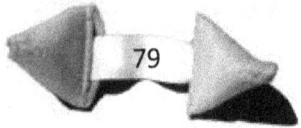

*Putting your
dreams
into a vessel
that is
too small
will never
allow
those dreams
to reach
its
full
potential*

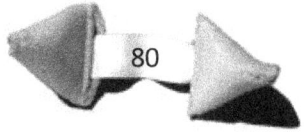

When dealing
in
value;
it is all about
the
margins,
what do you
gain
and
if the gain is
bigger than the
cost

81

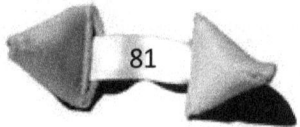

You should
never presume
to be so
sure
as to know
exactly
what
is
coming
around
the
next-corner

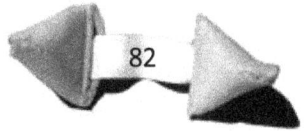

*No matter
what happens,
it is your
job
to
come
out
stronger
than
you
were
before*

In every and anything that you are involved with, you should always include the variables

84

*You should
always
keep in mind
that
no-one
will ever
be able
to
hear
what you
do not
say*

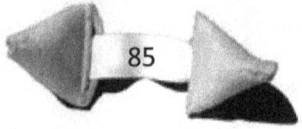

Situations
will
always
look
different
from a
leaders-seat
than
it would look
from the
rest
of the followers

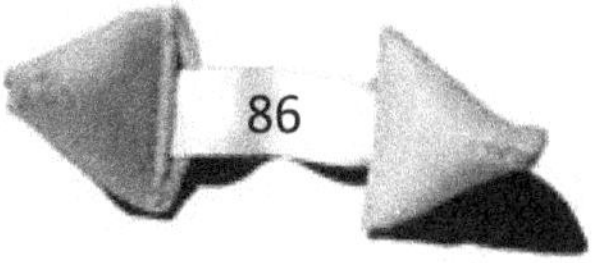

*When living
a
life
depending
upon
the
acceptance
of
others,
appearances
are
everything*

You will not
get
to
the
top
of
your
game
by
making
dumb
decisions

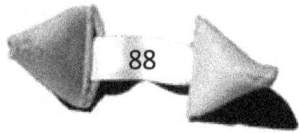

A dream and a desire to make a better life for yourself is what you will need in order to succeed

*Most times
it is all
about
imposing
your will
in order for you
to
achieve the
desired
outcome that
you would like
to achieve*

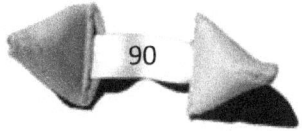

*It is
through the
constant
movement
towards
your
goal
that you will
achieve
success
in that
goal*

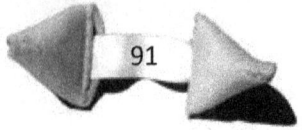

*Proper
planning
will
always
prevent
a
poor
performance*

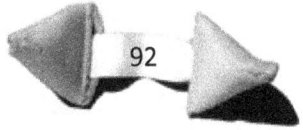

*The
only
true
road-blocks
that
you
can
ever
have
are
mental-ones*

*Each
step
accomplished,
moves
the
story
of
your
life
further
ahead*

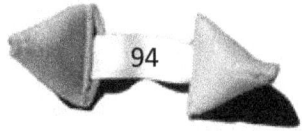

*Powerful
dreams
need
more
than
just
a
weekend
gardener*

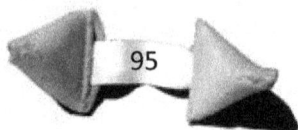

*The key
to making
an
individual
love
you
is a
mixture
of
absence
and
presence*

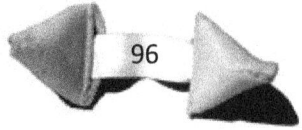

It will always
be
considered
a
disgrace
for you
to
let
your
talent
go to
waste

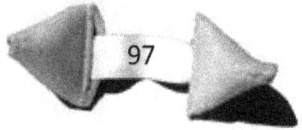

When you always keep in mind that a person's perspective comes from the life that they have lived, you will always have an deeper-insight to that person

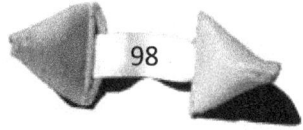

*Be wary
of
too
much
future
thinking
because
it
might
stagnate
your
current-flow*

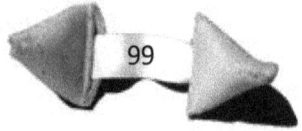

*In life you cannot
treat people the
way they are
supposed to be
treated,
although you
may want to; but
in its stead
you have to
treat them
how they are
accustomed
to being treated*

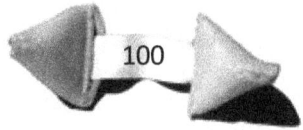

*Life
has a
malicious
way
of
dealing
with
great
potential
that
is
untended*

*The day
that
you stop
dreaming is the
day
that you
are
on a
path
to no
where;
extremely fast*

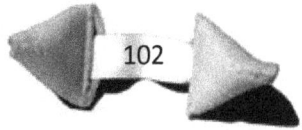

*Strategy
should
dictate
your
path,
not
the
other
way
around*

103

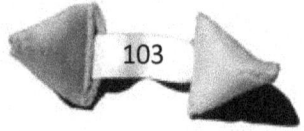

*If you don't
understand
the way
or
how a person
thinks,
then you
will not be able
to
anticipate
their
moves*

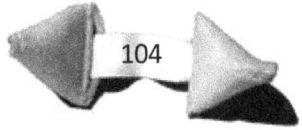

*What was
once stolen
in
heaps
and
piles
is not going
to be
recovered
all
at
once*

*Life
is
short,
enjoy
the
time
that
you
have
left*

When you
try
hard enough;
a
no
that you
continuously
run in to
can
become
a
yes

By the constant effort that you place into the attainment of your dreams, your dreams will better themselves

108

*It will
always
be too
late too
take
back
that
which
has
already
been
done*

You should never have the fear of tackling your problems head-on because most times it is the best-way to solve them

After accomplishing your short-term goals it is extremely wise to re-estimate all your original estimates

*Honoring
your belief
in who
you
would
like
to
become
should
be
your
everything*

112

*Every
quest
has
a
beginning
somewhere,
do not
be
ashamed
to
take
it*

113

*Always
remember
that
everyone
is
right
in
their
own
eyes*

*Often
times
big
dreams
and
accomplishments
will
start-off
small*

*Guilty
people
will
often
make
the
first
move,
pay
attention*

*Investing
in
yourself
is
investing
in
your
future*

*Just
because
it
happens
or
has
happened
does
not
mean that
it is
right*

When not paying attention to where you want to end-up in life, it is easy to go in the wrong-direction

*You will
always
be
remembered
by your
first
impression
so
always make it
an
outstanding
one*

*Results
will
always
speak
for
themselves*

*Keep in mind
that it is
difficult
for
people
to
stop
doing
what
wins
for
them*

123

Always remember that people are going to do what they feel like they have to do, regardless of what you advise them to do

There are often only three reasons why people will come into your life; for a reason, for a season, or for a lifetime and the sooner you figure out which one, the faster you will know where to place them

125

Be aware of the
fact that
your
life
can
become
better-off
without
certain
people
in
it

*Question
anything that
has something
to do
with you
because
it
never
hurts
to
be
safe*

*Learning
how
to
listen
to
your
own
voice
is
extremely
important*

When a person's actions is saying one-thing but their mouth is saying something different, that is the person you should not trust

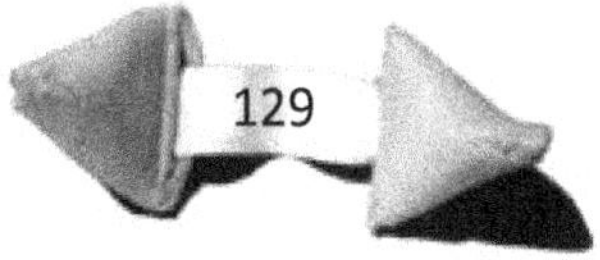

*Take
each
challenge
that
you
face,
one
step
at
a
time*

In whatever it is that your involved in, it is important not to get carried away and to always remember that you have too hold-on too you

131

*Learn to believe
in yourself and
know how to
change
with your
life,
and all the
things that you
desire
will
be
possible*

*Sometimes
there isn't
anything that
you can do
about certain
outcomes
and
you will just
have to
accept
the results
obtained*

*Remember that
when
you put people
into
teams,
you are
bound to have
personalities
that are
going
to
clash*

134

*If
you are going to
push forward
and
be
successful,
you must
weed-out
the
weak-links
in your
life*

You
can
never
get
anything
that
is
substantial
done,
without
of
planning

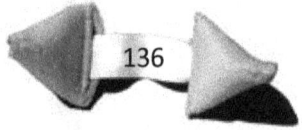

*It is important
to remember
that the
clothes
that
you
wear,
should be
like you
wearing
you
ability*

*It is important
to
realize that
what you are
doing is either
going to allow
you to be
all that you
can be
or
it is
not*

*It's not
fair
to expect
a piece
of the
cake
when
you are
unwilling
to help
bake
it*

Sometimes
you have
to
return
to
your
source
and
listen
to
your
inner-voice

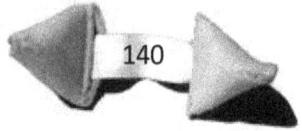

Keep in mind that when you are on the top, the only place for you to go is down so maintenance is extremely important in order to maintain your position

*Sometimes
in
life
you will
have to
take
two-steps
back
in order to
take
four-steps
forward*

Learn how
to
stand-up
for
yourself
because
once
pushed-around,
most
likely
always
pushed-around

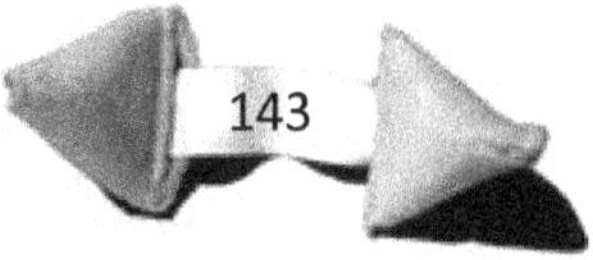

*Always keep in
mind
that in
life
sometimes
being
by
yourself
is
the
best-thing
for you*

*Learning how
to work
with the laws
of
attraction
and not against
them,
will work in
your best
interest of
obtaining
anything*

*Your life will
either be that
you do it all for
something
or that
you are doing it
all for nothing
and
you are the one
which makes
that
decision*

*Money
will
always
have
a
way
of
making
time
relevant*

Whenever
anyone
tries to do
a lot
in a little
bit of
time, an
accident
is
bound
to
happen

The only way
there is to
get-out
of
a
bad-deal
is
to
get-out
while
you
can

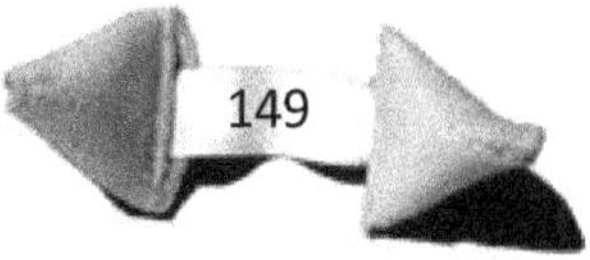

*You
should
always
think
twice
before
you
move
once*

Always remember that people only see the end-result, they never really see the whole-process of the things that you have done or are doing

The
people
that
get
things
done
do
not
need
excuses

152

The
mistakes
you
make
will
often
lead
you
to
a
new
discovery

*When
people are
overwhelmed
by
their
emotions,
there is
no
telling
how
they will
react*

*Always
remember
that
along
with
fun
comes
responsibility*

*If
you can
dream
it,
then
you
have
the
power
to
accomplish
it*

Remember that
most of the
people
in the
world
are
sheep,
they have
a
need to
be
lead

*Just remember
some people
were made
from a
different
kind
of
clay
than you
are
made
from*

*In this life you
should
want
to
do
something
that will
make
the
world
remember
you*

*Your future
constantly
changes
depending
upon the
choices
that
you choose
and the
decisions
that you
make*

The end

Additional books written by

Dr. Kareem Pottinger available online at

www.FORTUNECOOKIES.me

and your local book stores nationwide

FORTUNE COOKIES VOLUMES 1-11

also

available

on

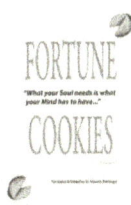
your

Kindle

Nook

Apple

devices